IF THESE ROOMS COULD TALK

IF THESE ROOMS COULD TALK

(A Compilation of the Wisdom I Have Heard

in the Rooms of Al-Anon)

By

Lois Charlene Forti

Copyright © by Lois Charlene Forti
© 2014 by Lois Charlene Forti – COPYRIGHT IN PROCESS
All rights reserved.
No parts of this publication can be reproduced or copied without the expressed written consent of the author.

Dedication

For my parents, Louis and Rosalie, who loved, accepted, and supported me their entire lives and who still guide me from above.

To my college sweetheart, my biggest fan, and the love of my life, my husband Richard. You have held my hand and been my best friend along this bumpy road and we did it together—always in love.

To my four incredible children—to whom I credit every lesson I have ever learned, and to their unique and loving spouses—thank you for being my spiritual teachers and for giving me the greatest joy in life, my beautiful grandchildren.

To all my Al-Anon sisters and friends who have shared my journey of self-discovery, you have my deepest gratitude for your friendship, your wisdom, your never-ending support, and your open hearts. We are blessed!

Table of Contents

Dedication v
Preface ix
Abuse 1
Acceptance 3
Advice, Learning, Teaching 7
Alcoholism, Addiction 11
Amends, Anonymity, Attitude 13
Anger 15
Change 17
Character Defects 21
Codependence 27
Courage 29
Denial, Control 33
Detachment 37
Faith 39
Fear 43
Focus on Yourself 47
Forgiveness 51
God 53
Gratitude 61
Happiness 63
Hope 65
Humor, Humility 69

Insanity of the Disease	71
Judgment	73
Let It Begin with Me	75
Living in the Moment	77
Love	81
Mind My Own Business	85
Miscellaneous	89
Negativism	93
Prayer	95
Resentment, Shame	97
Self-Love	101
Serenity Prayer	105
Serenity, Spirituality	107
Surrender	111
The Disease	113
The Journey, The Growth	115
The Program	121
The Twelve Traditions	127
Wisdom	135
Worry	143
Index	145

Preface

I came into these rooms in 1989. I remember because it was the same year I got my fur coat. It was a Christmas gift from my husband and he went through great effort to make a scavenger hunt out of my finding the present. The first clue appeared under the Christmas tree and directed me through several other rooms, closets, and hints until the huge, beautiful box was discovered in an upstairs hiding place. I guess he wanted to compensate for all the pain and sorrow that was occurring in our house at the time.

Our sixteen-year old child was using drugs and our lives were completely unmanageable. I wore that fur coat to my first meeting. It was January and I wrapped myself in the warmth of that lovely gift and sat in the back of the room. I came late and left early, before the closing, so I didn't have to speak to anyone. I don't know why, but by the Grace of God, I kept coming back and little, by slowly, I kept getting better.

• • •

That was over twenty-five years ago and a lifetime of learning has been granted to me since then. I think of who I was then and who I am now and I have the rooms and the people in the rooms to thank for that ever-evolving transformation. Many people have come into my life over these past twenty-five years—some briefly, some stayed for a little while, and some have been constant. All of them angels and teachers from God to help me along this learning and growing path. I don't remember them all, but some are still larger than life in my heart and my mind.

Dennis, soft spoken, hard of hearing, he would remove his hearing aids before he shared and then words of gentle comfort and spirituality would flow from him. His faith and wisdom were gifts he left with all of us when he moved to South Dakota to live with his only brother.

Lena—a small, short, feisty Italian lady whose "tell it like it is" attitude caught me by surprise one morning after a meeting when she approached me and said, "Girl, you better get off your pity pot—you're getting a big red welt around your ass from sitting there for so long!" Go Lena!

The three blonde, stereotypical New York ladies who marched into our home group one Wednesday morning and literally took over the meeting with their presence and Karma. They told me that life was like a game of poker (or "poka" as they said it!) and that I could throw in three cards. That I didn't have to play the hand I was dealt. "You got choices, girl, *choices*!" This was a new concept to me.

So many people pass through my mind from yesterday. Monica, the sweet, tall, curly haired redhead who found recovery in the rooms from the disease of alcoholism, but didn't win the battle with the cancer that took her life. We attended her funeral, her Al-Anon friends, and met her still-drinking husband. He was handsome, dapper, and perfect in front of all the mourners, but we knew the sorrow of her story.

Claudia, the young mother who suffered from MS and an alcoholic husband. Her disease was so advanced she struggled for every breath. She came for a while and then I guess life just got too difficult because we stopped seeing her. I still feel sad when I think of Claudia.

Josie. Sweet Josie who married her second husband well into her seventies, because he convinced her their love of music and dancing was a good foundation for marriage. He turned out to be an abusive, raging drunk. We would walk Josie to her car after each meeting because he was stalking her night and day and tried to keep her a prisoner in her own home. A restraining order proved futile as he walked up to her one Sunday afternoon while she peacefully listened to a summer concert on the green in her hometown and shot her through the head. He then took his own life. My heart still aches for Josie and her family.

Sue and her alcoholic husband found recovery ten years before he succumbed to a hard battle with cancer. She walked the widow path, trying to be strong and unable to know that that faithful day of September 11, 2001 would claim the life of her only son, a successful lawyer who worked at the World Trade Center. Four years later she would die of brain cancer. Sue . . . her journey was unthinkable.

Bruce—a big, rough, gruff pillar of the program. An old-timer, who corrected me every time I shared, criticized me every time I programmed, and scared the hell out of me for years. He was a throwback to the "no nonsense" days of the program and, scared or not, I learned a lot from Bruce. I was sad to watch him age and eventually pass.

Pat and I came into the program at the same time. We both had four kids and crazy families. She was everybody's "go to" girl—smart, walking the walk, and talking the talk. I'm still here, but we buried Pat after a long and painful battle with brain cancer. In the end, her Al-Anon Family was there for her—bringing her meals, taking her to doctor appointments, being vigilant at her bedside, and cherishing the time we had left with her. She was loved. She is missed.

These and countless others who came in and out of the rooms left their footprints on my heart. There was a woman, I can't recall her name, but I also can't forget her. She came every Wednesday morning—thin, drawn, leaning on her walker with an oxygen tube protruding from her nose, and her hair thinning more each week. She had a smile that defied her situation and she was like a breath of fresh air. I called her "my little Doe" because seeing her was a gift from God—a message of hope, like seeing a beautiful deer on the road after a long and hard day. A reminder of God and the beauty of His creations. I pray she is at peace today.

Corey. Young, sweet, loving, and giving Corey. She came into the rooms with one child and the women in our group immediately adopted her as our "daughter." Unbelievably, she shared three more pregnancies with us and we watched as she embraced recovery with a passion and commitment that was heartwarming. Her husband found sobriety and they took their little tribe to New York where they bought an old farmhouse with a barn where Corey opened two holistic businesses, home schools her little angels and, hopefully, lives in serenity. I always welcome the summer because sometimes, on an especially blessed Wednesday morning, Corey strolls into our meeting and surprises us by visiting her old "adopted" mothers.

So many people, so many voices, so much wisdom in these rooms. Finding Al-Anon has been the greatest discovery of my life. The program has been, at times, a parent, a sibling, a friend, a teacher, a lawyer, and a voice of reason in the dark hours. It has been my most trusted servant and the handbook to open when I am lost.

I have heard laughter, tears, sorrow, joy, anger, rage, and every other emotion known to man in these rooms, but mostly I have heard wisdom. Since day one I have written down pearls of wisdom, quotes and words that have struck a chord in my heart. I have kept journals of these gems and now it is time to share them with you, my friends. I have given credit to the person I am quoting whenever possible, but sometimes the wisdom will be unclaimed—just shared with you as it was shared with me.

I write this with gratitude and thanksgiving to you all and to give voice to the wisdom in the rooms of Al-Anon. If these rooms could talk, this is what they would say.

• • •

ABUSE

Abuse: First time a victim . . . Second time a volunteer.

People who feel good about themselves don't hurt other people.

When I get into negativity, I am abusing myself. (– Anna)

4 U's: If it is *unkind*, *unfair*, or *uncomfortable*, then it is *unacceptable*.

It only takes a few minutes to open gaping wounds and it takes years to heal them.

Get out of the line of fire. (– Mary C.)

Avoid the minefields of family relations.

Whenever we tolerate sick and inappropriate behavior we are responsible for the outcome.

Hurt people hurt people.

ACCEPTANCE

Wear life like a loose garment, not like a tight girdle. (– Jeri)

For those that understand, no explanation is necessary. For those who don't understand, no explanation is possible.
(– Jerry)

Whatever happens in life is a gift. You may not like the wrappings, but inside is a gift because life itself is a gift.

You can't get ahead if you are trying to get even.

Serenity is a perpetual quietness of the heart. (– Julie)

I've never been to a picnic that didn't have flies. (– Oren)

I have to "Let Go" of something to get to acceptance.

My acceptance is in direct proportion to my serenity.

What we resist persists.

Celebrate the best; forgive the rest. (– Corinne)

Lord, help me to accept, rather than *expect*.

Acceptance does not mean I have to acquiesce.

I can do anything for 12 hours that would appall me to do it for a lifetime.

The only thing you don't have to work at is being yourself.

I have serenity to the degree I have acceptance.

If I'm okay with me, I have no need to make you wrong.

Serenity is the door I want to pass through and acceptance is the key to opening that door.

I wanted the Brady Bunch and I got the Adams Family.

In acceptance lieth peace.

Acceptance is giving up all hope that I can have a better past.
(– Marsha)

If I can't accept, I'm intellectualizing.

You have to take the bitter with the better.

Silence gives acceptance.

Acceptance is seeing with your heart and not your eyes.

Acceptance gives me choices.

ADVICE, LEARNING, TEACHING

You give advice to others to interfere; you give advice to yourself to grow.

Our enemy is our teacher.

Time does not change us; it simply unfolds us.

Your vision will become clear only when you can look into your own heart.

Experience is what you get when you don't get what you want.

Wisdom is the reward we get from a lifetime of listening when we'd rather be talking. (– Moon)

"Figuring it out" is not one of our slogans. (– Moon)

The short version of the 12 steps, "Grow Up." (– Bibby)

People who are "Pains in the ass" are spiritual teachers. They teach me patience and kindness. (– Oren)

Believe your beliefs and doubt your doubts. (– Pam)

Don't let anyone "Should" all over you!

That which does not kill us makes us stronger.

A + B = C. Attitude plus behavior equals consequences.

When you know better, you do better and you feel better. (– Jane)

I am my own qualifier.

The opposite of success is not failure. The opposite of success is learning because when you fail, you learn. When you fail you fall forward to learn and grow. (– Marilyn)

If you've been there, no explanation is needed. If you haven't been there, than no explanation is sufficient. (– Chad)

The more you know about anything, the more likely you are to teach.

Two rules for dealing with stress:
1. Don't sweat the small stuff.
2. Don't sweat the small stuff.

If you learn better, you can do better. If you learn bigger, you can do bigger.

Don't major in minors!!

It's a small thing to a Giant. (– Eric)

Don't disregard the message because you don't like the messenger.

Be other-directed. Empathize; do not criticize.

Take my advice—I'm not using it! (– John)

ALCOHOLISM, ADDICTION

Anyone who is not an alcoholic or working hard to become one, never questions if they are an alcoholic!

Addiction is not being able to say "NO."

Addiction is a pathological relationship.

The disease does not operate in isolation.

In the disease of alcoholism, if you treat the alcoholic normal, they feel rejected. If you treat them special, they feel normal.

You are only as sick as your secrets.

As we let more people into our lives, we are that many relationships further away from a relationship with drugs and alcohol.

I thought I had a problem with drinking, but I had a problem with thinking. (– Ray)

Stinking thinking!

Alcohol kills the alcoholic and never giving up kills us.

Alcoholic Families learn three things: Don't talk, don't trust, and don't feel.

Alcoholism is not just a spectator sport; eventually every member of the family gets to participate.

AMENDS, ANONYMITY, ATTITUDE

People with tact have less to retract.

Anonymity takes all the joy out of gossip.

A good attitude is contagious.

PACE = Positive attitude changes everything.

Exchange PMS for PMA—Positive Mental Attitude

Attitude is the paintbrush of the soul.

One way to practice amends is to stop practicing the defeat.

Keeping it simple is getting rid of the unnecessary so the necessary can speak.

Your thoughts become attitudes. Your attitudes become behavior. Behavior becomes character. Your character becomes your destiny.

Making amends is responding differently, from a place of new understanding.

Alcoholism is 90% attitude and 10% Booze.

We in Ala-Anon have a dis-ease of attitude.

Attitude: A pilot's term for "angle of approach." The pilot must adjust his attitude (angle of approach) or the plane will lose its flight pattern and will be in danger. So, too, we need to adjust our attitude or angle of approach or we will be in spiritual trouble. (– Todd)

ANGER

No one wins the battle in which control is lost.

I don't need to attend every argument I am invited to; furthermore I don't even need to RSVP!

Using anger to solve a problem is like letting a fan take care of a pile of bills. (– Jim)

If you get to anger, put the "D" in front of it and stop—Danger.

He who angers you, controls you.

I can't converse when I am angry or afraid.

He who angers you conquers you and makes you a victim.
(– Madeline)

Anger is not getting what I want in the present.

Do not cultivate your own anger.

Anger today for me is sadness.

Most of the time, anger is a secondary emotion.

Anger + Shame = Rage

An overreaction is coming from some pain in the past.

Rage is an addiction.

Rage is mood altering.

Anger sits on a foundation of fear.

Once I've raised my voice, I've lost the argument.

Respond; don't react.

What starts in anger, ends in shame. (– Randy)

Hysteria is historical.

CHANGE

If you don't change, it doesn't change.

You don't need another person to make you whole—you just have to be that other person.

When the student is ready, the teacher arrives.

The pillars of my old identity will not support the weight of my recovery.

You can't go back to being a cucumber once you become a pickle. (– Corinne)

If you want to change, concentrate on the three C's:
Don't *criticize*, don't *complain*, and don't *condemn*.

If you always do what you always did, then you will always get what you always got!

Nothing changes, if nothing changes.

The past is a wonderful teacher, but that's all.

If I want to change the way I feel, then I need to change the way I act.

Say nothing, do nothing, change nothing.

No farmer ever plowed a field by turning it over in his mind.

Life comes from inside—if you change internally then you can enjoy the outside.

If a relationship dies, I do not have to die along with it.

My choices reflect my opinion of a relationship with myself.

Somehow we try to change other people to fit into what we want instead of fitting ourselves into what God wants us to be.

My conditioning is stronger than my intellect.

In the looking there is so much learning. (– Liz)

Experience is an amazing teacher. (– Roxy)

Comfortably uncomfortable (– Suzanne)

What didn't you understand about the word "No," the "N" or the "O?"

CHARACTER DEFECTS

An egomaniac has an inferiority complex.

I am my own roadblock.

Shortcoming—falling short of a goal.

Stop being a human doing and start being a human being.

There is many a sip between the cup and the lip.

If you have a constant need to help someone, then you have a constant need to keep someone helpless.

Few people live up to their reputation when you get up close and personal to them.

If two people never disagree, one person is unnecessary.
(– Jane)

Be alert to God's coming and be patient with your shortcomings. (– Fr. Ed)

Self-doubt is a defeat of character.

I had a massive ego but absolutely no self-esteem. (– Dennis)

We all carry a little black box containing all our genetic maladies. Stress is the key that opens that black box.

When you are nailing behavior, make sure it is not character assassination. (– Michelle)

The choices we make in life are directly related to our self worth. (– Lisa)

Habits can be cork or lead—they can hold you up, or weigh you down.

There is no such thing as a healthy extreme.

The foundation was always there—I've burned down many houses, but the foundation remained. (– Barry)

People don't change what they feel—they learn to conceal.

Only secure, confident people can be truthful.

A slip is losing myself totally.

When we listen as carefully to the self-image as we listen to the self-critic, we discover we are capable of the insurmountable.
(– Louise)

Be a wall breaker—not a ball breaker!

Overachievers are driven by shame.

I am hardwired with this disease. (– Heather)

ISM = In Side Mess.

My character defects are really the taproot to my spirituality.
(– Charlie)

I am a sick person getting well, not a bad person getting good.
(– Charlie)

How easy it is to hurt those we know so well, whose every weakness is familiar, whose soft spots are exposed. (– Zach)

A habit is a habit—not to be kicked, but to be coaxed downstairs, one step at a time.

By judging others we display the shortcomings in ourselves.

When I try to get even, I get even sicker.

Are you prepared to be repaired?

How does my unmanageable life qualify me to manage your unmanageable life? (– Oren)

People with dirty feet dance in my head, if I let them. (– Kathy)

I suffer from the 4 M's: Mothering, Magnification, Managing, and Martyrdom.

Expectations are premeditated resentments.

Imperfection does not signify worthlessness. (– Maurice)

Don't create a crisis, but don't avert a crisis in the natural progression of things.

We don't trip on mountains; we trip on the small stones getting to the mountains. (– Ray)

Move from Judgment into Enlightenment

Being right for the wrong motives is still wrong.

Being right all the time is such a burden.

I'm allergic to pain in anyone else's life—I want to fix it. (– Andrew)

CODEPENDENCE

You don't have to ride every garbage truck to the dump.

I have the thermometer in your mouth, trying to determine how I'm feeling. (– Helen)

The Silver Rule: Don't do for others what they can do for themselves. (– Julie)

A friend is someone who shares your truth.

I am powerless over mood-altering people. (– Oren)

Being a Martyr is a character flaw.

By giving another person their freedom, you give yourself your freedom.

The depths of the ocean are undisturbed by the waves above it.

It's okay to Mother, but not to *smother*.

Healthy relationships are out of Want, not out of Need.

Our loved ones don't make our lives, but loving them does.

Don't compare your insides with someone's outsides.

COURAGE

The only way out is through.

In order to heal the pain you have to go through the pain.

Pain is the nutcracker that breaks the shell of understanding.
(– Roberta)

Courage is fear that has said its prayers.

Courage is born of humility.

Hang in, Hold on, and Let Go. (– Jane)

Survival is a bottoming-out process.

Out of survival comes growth and new life.

I can allow the people in my life to soar or roar—that is giving them their dignity.
(– Anna F.)

Positive thinking without positive action is nothing.

When you're lying in the ashes of life you have two choices: you can get up or give up.

If your head can conceive it and your heart can believe it, your hands can achieve it.

The toughest challenges lead to the greatest triumphs.

We need an alarm clock that will ring when it is time for us to rise to the occasion.

Hesitation and Procrastination keep you from your Destination.

Delaying obedience is disobedience.

Defeat is the Devil's password.

The secret to getting ahead is to get started.

Wear life like a loose garment. (– Patrick)

Keep your chin up—it's easier to see heaven that way.

This is the only disease in the world where you can kill someone with kindness.

Don't be defeated by opposition. Remember a kite rises against the wind.

Walk in courage and faith, not fear and despair.

Do I live by chance or by choice?

If I never say "No," what is the value of my "Yes?"

Live by design, not by chance.

Courage is the price that life exacts for granting peace.
(– Maurice)

DENIAL, CONTROL

Before the light can shine through the windows, the blinds need to be raised.

Jewish Proverb: Nobody sees their own hunchback. (– Roy)

Enabling causes lack of self-esteem. (– Jim)

I spot what I got!

Helping is the sunny side of control. (– Oren)

Control is the product of our own insecurity.

Control is an illusion.

Denial is like sleeping—you don't know you are asleep until you wake up!

Micromanagers are suffocaters.

The "stuff" we don't deal with becomes an angry dog in the basement. (– Bob A.)

As far as you distance yourself from your pain, that's as far as you are from your joy. (– Bob A.)

The more you conceal, the more you don't heal.

The opposite of control is Growth.

Control: Blocks other people's growth.
Stops events from happening naturally.
Prevents us from enjoying people and life.

Once we've raised our voice we have lost the argument.

Silence gives blessing.

Control and Guidance come from God.

Obstacles are things people see when they take their eyes off their goals.

By yielding, you obtain victory.

Surrender means going over to the winning side.

Denial is not protection; Denial is a prison.

If I try to control, I circumvent God. (– Mike)

No one wins the battle when control is lost.

We can makeover or remodel our homes but not the people in our homes.

Our "will" spills out of eyes in the form of tears. (– Gwen)

We control in order to feel safe.

First time I say it, it is for information.
Second time I say it, it is for clarification.
Third time I say it, it is nagging and controlling. (– Oren)

DETACHMENT

Detachment never means disinterest or disgust.

Detachment means self-preservation

Detach for growth and survival.

Sometimes the best way to help is not to. (– Bob)

If you can't detach, hang loose. (– Elaine)

Detaching is not reacting. (– Jim)

Detach from your problem and attach to your higher power.

Enabling other people to do what they do to me is allowing them to continue to participate in their unhealthy behavior. (– Nick)

Detachment helps me to let go of my loved one's behavior and words.

The greatest gift I can give myself is my own attention.

Detachment is not a wall; it is a bridge. (– Rasheed)

Detaching with compassion is to give dignity to that person.

FAITH

To live in the now in faith is surrender. (– Oren)

Making mistakes has been part of my spiritual awakening.

Trust in the process.

Life is to be honored, not solved.

Faith will take you places that reason won't. (– Dennis)

Faith is the bird that sings when the dawn is still dark.

There are two answers to prayer: "Yes" and "I have something better for you." (– Jane)

If I feed my faith, my fears will starve to death.

Faith is Divinity being transmitted through the weakness and frailty of man.

I wish you the highest vision that God has for your life to become a reality.

You can't put in what God has left out.

The spirit is given so we can go from a place of *nothing* to a place of Wealth.

Differences are an invitation to the openness of the spirit of God. (– John)

We allow Faith to overpower our thoughts, if we are people of faith. (– John)

Only the person who has faith in himself is able to be faithful to others.

Faithfulness means both sorrow and joy.

The opposite of fear is faith.

P.U.S.H. = Pray Until Something Happens.

The greatest act of Faith is in knowing you are not God.
(– Kathy)

I have unshakable Faith, but it comes and goes! (– Oren)

Faith activates God; Fear activates the devil.

FEAR

F.E.A.R. = Forgetting Everything Is Alright

F.E.A.R. = False Evidence Appearing Real

My batting average is 2% . . . 98% of what happens, actually happens in my head. (– Oren)

Living in fear is a contradiction of terms.

Fretting and worrying about a problem does not count as action. (– Oren)

Fear is "not getting what I want in the future."

Most of our worries are reruns!

The other side of fear is faith.

F.E.A.R. = Face Everything And Recover

I can understand why a child is afraid of the darkness; what I don't understand is why an adult is afraid of the light.

Fear can't go where faith resides. (– Terry)

Fear and Faith can't live in the same heart.

Depression is the impression left by fear. (– The Forum)

The antidote for fear is faith.

Fear is the dark room where the devil takes us to develop our negatives!

When I get to a place of panic, I know I am void of a higher power and of my program. (– Stephanie)

The greatest of our fears shows the smallness of our faith.

Our fear defeats the causes of God.

A frozen heart won't feel pain.

I know when fear walks in, my faith has walked out.

Fear is self-centered.

If fear were money, we would all be millionaires.

Fear is not living in the Now.

FOCUS ON YOURSELF

I AM the priority. (– Andy)

He who wanders in someone else's mind is totally lost.
(– Jackie)

Life is a do-it-yourself project.

Happiness is an inside job.

Am I carrying the disease or am I carrying the message?

Give of your excess, not of your essence.

Get busy living or get busy dying. (– Tony at his 1st meeting)

Keep up your RPM's: Read, Pray, Meditate. (– Janine)

Let "them" run their own lives, even if they run it into a wall.
(– Jerry)

Mother may know best, but only just for Mother.

You can't go wrong doing the right thing.

Loving yourself is a lifelong romance.

If you're having trouble with your outlook, you better have an *in look*. (– Sue G.)

Our first order of business is to ourselves.

Admitting our weakness allows us to be strong in the broken places.

The space that needs to be expanded is our inner space.

Solitude is not toxic—it is nurturing and intimate.

LAF = Love, Accept, Forgive

Have a voice—go on record for yourself.

The beauty of God's Child is within.

The worst loneliness is not to be comfortable with yourself.

In my living of today, I cannot accommodate the fears, feelings, and wants of other people. I need to be true to myself.
(– Dennis)

Failure can be the back door to success.

Intimacy means "In To Me SEE."

Keep the focus on myself. It is where everything begins and where everything ends.
(– Jean)

FORGIVENESS

Forgiveness is not forgetting. It is letting go of the hurt.

Forgiveness does not mean reconciliation.

You can forgive a man for murdering your daughter, but you don't invite him back to babysit your son. (– Liz)

In a family, there is no crime beyond forgiveness.

Forgiveness is an act of will.

Forgiveness is for you, not the other person.

Forgiveness of our selves is where all forgiveness starts.

Celebrate the best—forgive the rest. (– Corinne)

Forgiveness is not about exonerating the other person; it is about empowering your self.

Forgiveness is about exhaling—Let it go!

Forgiveness is letting go and moving on.

Forgiveness is the act of setting a prisoner free and the prisoner is you. (– Elaine)

By not forgiving, I am held hostage by that person.

Forgiveness is a reminder that I am on equal footing with every other child of God.

Forgiveness allows space in our lives for our own healing.

Forgiveness is the remedy for resentments.

GOD

Through my handicaps, I have found my love, my life's work, and my God. (– Helen Keller)

God is to be found in the very core of every moment—whether it is joy or pain. (– John)

The Twelve Steps are God's telegram to us—telling us how to live our lives.

Let go and Let God or hang on and get dragged.

I can't. He can. I think I'll let Him!

God: loving, kind, slow to anger, and abounding in fidelity.

There are no coincidences—only " Godincidences."

If you worry, why pray? If you pray, why worry? (– Liz)

E G O = Easing God Out

Impatience is man's attempt to interrupt God's divine plan.

Sleep well tonight, God is awake.

God has no Stepchildren or Grandchildren; He only has Children.

Most of the chaos in my life today is caused by trying to diffuse God's plan. (– Mike)

Flowers and animals are God's apology for the rest of the world. (– Lynn)

Coincidences are God's little miracles that he doesn't take credit for.

God's voice is as loud as my willingness to listen.

We find God in our insufficiency.

God is ever present in his absence.

From the visible we come to an understanding of the invisible.

We are restless until our hearts rest in God.

The best sermon is a good example.

No one circumstance is your source of supply. God is. (– Gayle)

God will never do for you or do to you, but He will work with you and through you. (– Chad)

The tragedy is not to live a short life; the tragedy is to live a long life and never live it in relationship to God.

God never hurries, but he is never late. (– Sylvia)

We can't see around the corners, but God can. (– Maurice)

3 G's: Get out of God's Way.
       Get off His back.
       Get on with your life.

Pain is God's reset button.

The Lord will never lead you where His grace can't reach you.

God supplies, we apply.

Sometimes man's rejection is God's protection.

Not to use the blessings God has given us is to wait for internal combustion to destroy us.

Turn it over—you can't concentrate on God and your problems at the same time.

The hand of God is the bottom and when you hit the bottom the Palm of God is holding you. (– John)

God is found in the struggle. (– John)

When you can't trace the hand of God, trust the heart of God. (– John)

The thorn in our side is where God can make us strong. (– John)

I believe there is something greater than myself that makes the world pregnant with possibilities. (– John)

G U T = God Uttering Truth

Tearing down and building up again is always the way God asks us to change, empowered by His spirit. (– John)

Lord, help me to accept, rather than expect.

God's voice is as loud as my willingness.

G A P = God Always Provides

God picked me up in a terrible place and I know when He drops me off it will be at a much better place. (– Kathy)

Perfection will come when you look eyeball to eyeball with the Lord. (– Maurice)

Others are the topsoil, but God is the root. (– Maurice)

God blesses our effort—He is not concerned with success or failure.

God is always found in the NOW.

We may not have it all together, but together we have it all.

God doesn't make junk!

Going to a meeting is praying with my feet. (– Oren)

God promises a safe landing—not a calm passage.

In His will is our peace. (– Dante-ODAT)

God relieve me of the bondage of self. (– Alfreda)

All is in perfect order in God's plan.

God comes disguised as your life.

Father, they are thine as I am thine. Please bring peace between us. (– Ray)

The nicest place to be is in someone's thoughts. The safest place to be is in someone's prayers. And the best place to be is in the hands of God.

Whatever I concentrate on will become my life.

When you know yourself, you know who your creator is.

The spirit of my God lives and speaks in all the faces and voices in these rooms.

My higher power shows up often in an unfamiliar face.

God doesn't ask me to accept life, that's not our choice. He asks us to learn from it.

I don't know what is best for others, because I don't know what lessons God is trying to teach them.

Guidance = God & I dance!

My blessing is in my attitude.

If it comes from the heart, it goes to the heart.

GRATITUDE

Gratitude is the awareness of God, alive and working in my life. (– Jane)

Write it on your heart that everyday is the best day of the year.

Gratitude is a choice.

Have an attitude of Gratitude.

Keep my expectations low and my gratitude high.

Today is the most important day of your life because it is the only day you have for sure.

So much has been given to me that I have not time to ponder what has been denied. (– Helen Keller)

No Day Is Promised.

Yesterday is a canceled check. Tomorrow is a mystery. Today is your treasure.

I am too blessed to be stressed and too anointed to be disappointed.

From Gratitude comes Joy.

Gratitude is a builder, a builder of good thinking and good living.

Gratitude is the cornerstone of my recovery.

Gratitude is the antidote for self-pity.

HAPPINESS

Happiness grows out of doing the next right thing. (– George)

Happiness is an inside job.

Happiness is a do-it-yourself project.

We are as happy as we make up our minds to be. (– Abe Lincoln)

Today I don't have to be right. Today I choose to be happy.

At this stage of my life it is more important for me to respect myself than to be liked. (– Taffy)

Happiness is the result of doing the next best thing to maintain my reality.

As deep as the Pain goes, that is as deep as the Joy. (– Birdie)

Happiness is not the absence of conflict; Happiness is the ability to cope with conflict. (– Alice)

You day goes the way the corners of your mouth turn.

Happiness is a decision.

Joy is to us what sunshine is to plants.

We can't cure the world of sorrow but we can choose to live in joy.

I get all my needs. I just don't always get all my wants.
(– Rosemary)

Pain and Joy often co-exist side by side. (– Doris)

Laughter is the solvent for self-pity. (– Shannon)

Happiness is a birthright.

HOPE

The situation for a miracle is difficulty; the situation for a really big miracle is impossibility.

What is meant for me will never get past me. (– Laura)

The Joy is in the Journey. (– Laura)

Life is a journey, not a destination.

H O P E = Holding Onto Positive Energy

Triumph is just a little "umph" added to "try."

My future has no room for the past.

Out of the darkness come the stars.

It never gets darker than midnight.

When we let go of a character defect, grace comes in to fill that empty hole. (– Elizabeth)

Don't be defeated by opposition; Remember, a kite rises against the wind.

There is a difference between pain and healing pain.

Nothing is the end of the world, but the end of the world.

Remember the ship won't sink and the storm won't last forever.

The greatest test of courage is to bear defeat without losing heart.

H O P E = Honesty, Openness, Prayer, Encouragement

Hope comes at every meeting just by comparison shopping.

Where there is help there is hope.

Where there is life there is hope.

Openness is to healing, as secrets are to sickness.

3 H's: Health, Happiness, Hope

No one can go back and make a brand new start, but we all can go back and make a brand new end. (– Claire)

Loss of hope is the undertaker's best friend. (– Maurice)

Failure can be the back door to success.

A diamond is a lump of coal made beautiful under pressure.

Hope deferred makes the heart sick.

Don't die with the diagnosis.

Have Hope—Stay Afloat.

Don't give up five minutes before the miracle happens.

Loss of hope is the worst possible loss.

Hope is the stimulus to action.

In the end, everything will be all right; and if it's not, it's because it's not yet the end.

Old Persian saying: Crystal Rain falls from dark clouds.

I am not afraid of the storms because I am learning to sail my own ship.

H O P E = Hang On, Pain Ends. (– Jim)

My Hope is fortified by going to a meeting.

The past is where you learn the lesson. The future is where you apply the lesson—don't give up in the middle. (– Linda)

Troubles are opportunities to grow.

Troubles can make us better—not bitter.

H O P E = Having Open Palms Extended

HUMOR, HUMILITY

When you live with turkeys it is sometimes hard to soar like an eagle. (– Roy)

Humility is *teach-ability*.

Humility is maturity.

Humility is the ability for me to accept God's will.

Sarcasm comes from the Greek word meaning, "to tear the flesh."

Smile—it increases your face value.

The Hallmark of self-esteem is Humility. (– Dennis)

We are all created human and in that creation we are perfect—perfectly human. (– Maria)

INSANITY OF THE DISEASE

Don't go upstairs without adult supervision. (– Oren)

We are all here because we are not all there!

The mind is a dangerous neighborhood—don't go in there alone.

My brain is like the hurricane warnings . . . It's a projected path of uncertainty.

I'm a slow learner and a fast forgetter. (– Oren)

Addiction is self will run riot.

Believing that I can change another person is insanity.

Doing the same thing over and over again and expecting different results is the definition of insanity.

Don't go to the hardware store for bread.

JUDGMENT

Don't compare my insides with someone else's outsides.

When you look inside yourself, you should see the face of God looking back.

I do not need to ask for forgiveness unless I have first judged and condemned you.

Education before evaluation

Principles above personalities

You spot what you got.

I see the speck in my brother's eye but miss the plank in my own.

When you point a finger at me, you are actually pointing three back at yourself.

Do not point at my spot until you have first cleaned your own finger.

Judge not and be thyself not judged.

Take only your own inventory

God is the only scorekeeper.

LET IT BEGIN WITH ME

I see what I am looking for.

I can't see with my eyes shut tight!

I am not responsible for anyone's actions or reactions.

An unexamined life is not worth living.

An examined life is not easily lived.

The worst vice is advice.

Speak without offending; Listen without defending.

Recovery is being authentic.

Someone else's opinion of me is none of my business.

The purpose of conversation is to engage, not enrage.

I am moved from criticism to love, when I look at my kids and loved ones.

Whoever is out of patience is out of his soul. Men must not turn into bees who kill themselves in order to hurt others.
(– Jonathan Swift)

No one can make you feel inferior without your consent.

If it is to be, it is up to me.

If you want milk, you can't sit in the middle of a field on a stool waiting for the cow to back up to your bucket.

Energy flows where attention goes. (– Oren)

I want to be proactive, not reactive.

I should try to run it through my Al-Anon filter, before I act or speak.

Honor is what I do when no one is looking. (– Allison)

You're your problem and you're your solution.

The more you obsess, the less productive you become. (– John)

Behave in a recovery manner. (– Rebecca)

Focus on the solution, not the problem.

Our attitudes are our emotional responses.

Don't get into analysis paralysis.

Minds are like parachutes—they function only when open.

I am a designer original!

You can't grow and go forward if you keep going back and tearing up your roots.

If the only tool you have in your toolbox is a hammer, then everything looks like a nail.

I can't think my way into right action; I have to act my way into right action.

People can be as responsible in their lives as I need to be in mine, if I just let them go.
(– Linda)

It's never too late to be a role model for your children.
(– Maureen)

Discipline puts death to your will.

Live and Let Live—But Live First.

Genuine intimacy involves a willingness to change and grow.

Intimacy is a partnership, not a merger.

Isolation is defending my right to hate.

Whatever the past may be, my future is spotless.

LIVING IN THE MOMENT

Grief demands that we live in the NOW.

To live in the NOW is to be in alignment with life.

The NOW is sacred.

The greatest transformations of life are embedded in the pain, the hurt, and the struggles of life. (– John)

To live in the NOW in faith is surrender. (– Oren)

Wherever you are—be there! (– Dana)

Life is what happens when we make plans.

Yesterday is a cancelled check. Tomorrow is a promissory note. Today is the only cash you have—spend it wisely.

Keep your head when your feet are.

Look back, but don't stare.

If you have one foot in tomorrow and one foot in yesterday you are pooping on today.

Yesterday is History. Tomorrow is a Mystery.

A fool will lose tomorrow looking at yesterday. (– Bob)

Live in the solution, not the problem.

If we fill our hours with regrets of yesterday and with worries of tomorrow, we have no today in which to be thankful.

Feelings are created by thoughts.

Remember Yesterday, Dream of Tomorrow, Live for Today.

Everyday is a gift from God, that is why it is called the Present.

I live my today's in the realm of eternity. (– Isabelle)

Today will be my past tomorrow.

The past is a foreign country—they do things differently there.

LOVE

What we give time to is what we love.

Trust is an attribute of Love.

When I get into negativity, I am not loving myself. (– Anna)

In every relationship there is love and there is pain. When the pain becomes greater than the love, the relationship ceases to be. (– Alberta)

Until death do us part; when the relationship dies, we need to part. (– Maurice)

I don't have to ever apologize to another person for taking care of myself. My goal today is to love myself as much as God loves me. (– Ellen)

Love is the only thing we can carry with us when we go.

Honesty without love is brutality. (– Mary C.)

No one cares how much you know, until they know how much you care.

When the power of love overcomes the love of power then—and only then—shall we have peace.

Peace at any price is not Love.

When Love is felt, the message is heard.

Small things done with great love become great things.

Love is a soft virtue. (– John)

We can't take the pain away from another person but we can be in that space with them and just love them. (– Alfreda)

I focus on the things outside myself, when I am not taking care of me. (– Anna)

Only love can transform pain. (– Thomas)

Love can't pass through a heart filled with resentment and fear.

It is impossible to run out of love.

No one who loves you would ever ask you to be anyone except who you are.

Self-love is to ask yourself daily: "What is life giving for me today?"

When I am respecting myself, I don't have to disrespect you.

MIND MY OWN BUSINESS

I find more courage today in keeping my mouth shut than I ever did in saying it.

Unsolicited advice is interference. (– Roy)

When I am getting my ducks in a row, I need to make sure they are my ducks!

Clean up my own side of the street.

If I'm taking inventory, it better be my own inventory.

If it's not in my hula hoop, it's not my business. (– Oren)

The wrong three words are: "Why don't you." (– Jackie)

I don't need to pour gasoline on the fires in my kid's lives.

I am the gatekeeper of my mind. (– Roy)

Hoe your own row! (– Jerry)

I'm just a bit player in other people's lives. (– Jack)

I create this whole elaborate play and assign each loved one a part, set the stage, produce and direct it, and when no one wants to play along I get angry at them??

Sometimes I'm so busy living in other people's heads that there's no one home in my own head.

You can't get ahead if you're trying to get even.

People with tact have less to retract.

No one likes another person to run interference, unless you are playing football.

Don't sweep my side of the street onto someone else's.
(– Kathy)

Never pass up an opportunity to keep your mouth shut.
(– John)

It is better to keep quiet and be thought a fool, than to open your mouth and remove all doubt.

Anytime I verbally interfere, I come away feeling less than. (– John)

Sometimes, in a chorus, there are enough voices without me adding mine. (– Ron)

If you are into problem solving, make sure the problem you are solving is your own. (– Anita)

We should have much peace if we do not busy ourselves with the doings and saying of others.

Communication:
    Does it need to be said?
    Does it need to be said by me?
    Does it need to be said right now?

95% of all resentments can be avoided if I just mind my own business.

Clean your own finger before you point at my spots. (– Ben Franklin)

MISCELLANEOUS

If you understand things are what they are, or if you don't understand things are what they are—things still are what they are!

Self worth is like water—it seeks its own level. (– Jane)

Suffering leads to endurance; Endurance leads to character; Character leads to Hope; and Hope does not disappoint.

Prudence means wisdom with balance.

Thoughts become words; Words become actions; Actions become behavior; and Behavior becomes our character.

It's always best to be a consultant in someone else's life, because if you're wrong, you have no responsibility, and if you're right, you take all the credit. (– Oren)

Victims don't recover.

S O B E R = Son of a Bitch—Everything is Real!

Life is so paradoxical— it is like one huge oxymoron.
(– Tiffany)

Passive aggressive is like a big St. Bernard Dog who licks your face and urinates on you at the same time.

Actions become patterns or bad habits.

Responsibility is the ability to respond to any situation.
(– Tiffany)

Becoming a healthy parent is never untimely. (– Maureen)

The mind is a bad neighborhood, never go in there alone, and take someone else for safety. (– Claire)

It's not what you call me, but what I answer to that counts.

A sponge that is saturated is no good and so is a dry sponge. (– Barry)

The Chinese Characters for the word "Crisis" are: Danger and Opportunity.

It is precisely in our weakness that we become strong. (– John)

No is a complete sentence.

Stick with the winners and win with the stickers.

You don't know what you don't know.

Never trouble trouble until trouble troubles you.

Troubles are often the tools by which God fashions us for better things.

If "it's" and "buts" were fruits and nuts, what a sweet world it would be. (– Juanita)

I can be helpful, if I am healthy.

An idea is nothing, until it is an action.

Miracles happen every day, but only one day at a time. (– Gail)

I need to let go because holding on is adding to my loved one's pain and making them more of a victim.

Other people's pain is controlling me!!!!

Psychological time is the time of the past and the time of the future—where all anxiety happens.

Time will always have a purpose.

Who is more foolish, the fool or the fool that follows? (– Mia)

NEGATIVISM

Murmuring is the language of defeat.

You can't grow and go forward if you keep going back and tearing up the roots.

To despair is to turn your back on God.

If you compare, you despair.

Exchange PMS for PMA = Positive Mental Attitude.

Don't judge the day by the weather.

When I am depleted, everyone can hurt my feelings. (– Mags)

My perspective determines my thoughts and my thoughts determine everything else. (– Kathy)

As I look back on my life, every time I thought I was being rejected from something good, I was actually being redirected to something better. (– Katie)

Being negative is just a lack of effort because being positive takes a lot of energy. (– Paul)

PRAYER

Your life is a prayer.

Prayer is just two hearts, your and God's, spending time together.

A song, a baby's cry, a kind word, a thing of beauty—all these things are a prayer to their creator.

A day woven together in prayer does not unravel. (– Oren)

God, thank you for what you've given me.
Thank you for what you've taken from me.
Thank you for what you've left me. (– Marilyn)

Dear God: For all that came before—Thank you.
For what is yet to come –YES! (– Bill S.)

Prayer is my Antidote.

Prayer is my Foundation.

There is no peace without prayer.

The teacher of Meditation and Prayer is Silence.

Every good thought is a form of prayer.

P U S H – Pray Until Something Happens. (– Jean)

RESENTMENT, SHAME

Resentment is the only thing that destroys its container.

S H A M E = Should Have Already Mastered Everything
(– Tina)

Resentment is not getting what I wanted in the past.

Removal of a defect does not remove the "inclination" of that defect. We have the choice to use that defect or not.

Holding onto resentment is allowing someone you despise to live rent-free in your brain.

The core of addiction is shame.

Self-pity slides very quickly into resentment and blame.

Healthy shame is: knowing your limits.

Healthy shame is permission to be human.

Shame is the basis of addiction.

The tragedy of shame is trying to be more than human or trying to be less than human.

Toxic shame leads to bankruptcy.

When you shame someone, you kill their soul.

Expectations are premeditated resentments.

The only way to heal the shame is to embrace the shame.

You will never get ahead if you are trying to get even.
(– Richard)

Tumors are malignant resentments.

Guilt is the ego's orgasm. (– Nancy)

The only difference between being in a rut, and being in a grave—are the dimensions.

Envy is a hostile form of self-pity.

All of us need recognition, but the less we like our selves, the more we need recognition.

Itty, Bitty, Shitty, Pity

Healthy shame is permission to be human.

Moral shame is guilt.

Toxic shame fuels addiction.

Secrets lose their shame when spoken in the light.

My mind was like Grand Central Station and finally I figured out that I didn't have to run to catch every damn train. (– Alex)

Resentments don't serve me well today; they rob my peace.

Resentments are like peeing down your own leg—you're the only one who feels it.

Do Not Brood over injury. (– 1ˢᵗ Corinthians, Ch.13)

Resentments are a defect of character.

Resentments hold no value to the human spirit.

Resentments are deep-seeded anger.

Resentments are like hemorrhoids—they only hurt the ass that has them.

SELF-LOVE

Self-love is . . . acknowledging and praising yourself.

Self-love is . . . having confidence in your ability

Self-love is . . . giving yourself pleasure, without the guilt.

Self-love is . . . loving your body and admiring your beauty.

Self-love is . . . giving yourself what you want and deserve.

Self-love is . . . letting yourself win.

Self-love is . . . letting others in.

Self-love is . . . following your intuition.

Self-love is . . . making your own rules, responsibly.

Self-love is . . . seeing your own perfection.

Self-love is . . . taking credit for your accomplishments.

Self-love is . . . surrounding yourself with beauty.

Self-love is . . . letting yourself be rich.

Self-love is . . . creating an abundance of friends.

Self-love is . . . rewarding yourself—never punishing yourself.

Self-love is . . . trusting yourself.

Self-love is . . . nourishing yourself with good food and good ideas.

Self-love is . . . surrounding yourself with people who nourish you.

Self-love is . . . enjoying making love.

Self-love is . . . getting a massage frequently.

Self-love is . . . seeing yourself as equal to others.

Self-love is . . . forgiving yourself.

Self-love is . . . having fun.

Self-love is . . . turning negative thoughts into affirmations.

(– By Terry)

SERENITY PRAYER

God, grant me the serenity to accept the things I cannot change;
The Courage to change the things I can;
And the wisdom to know the difference.

Living one day at a time;
Enjoying one moment at a time;
Accepting hardships as the pathway to peace;
Taking, as He did, the sinful world as it is,
not as I would have it;

Trusting that He will make all things right
If I surrender to His Will.
That I may be reasonably happy in this life,
And supremely happy with Him forever in the next.

Amen.

(– By Reinhold Niebuhr)

SERENITY, SPIRITUALITY

Serenity is like gravity—you can't see it, you can't touch it, but you can sure feel it.

My serenity is in direct proportion to my acceptance.

I don't need to feed my depression, but I do need to feed my happiness. (– Sam)

Religion is for people who are afraid of hell; Spirituality is for people who have lived in hell.

People who are spiritual have their souls tested in the dark of night.

Sin is self-destructing. Virtue is self-fulfilling.

My serenity is in direct proportion to my Letting Go.

Expectations will dilute my serenity.

Serenity is a calm appraisal of reality.

I am not a human being trying to have a spiritual experience—I am a spiritual being trying to become human. (– Steve)

Serenity is not freedom *from* the storm; it is freedom in the *midst* of the storm. (– Dennis)

Spirituality is living life on life's terms.

Serenity is not the absence of problems, but rather the presence of God. (– Maurice)

Spirituality is our relationship to Love.

To be all that we are capable of being is the height of spirituality. (– Maurice)

There is a spiritual reason for everything.

Sin is simply an error in judgment.

One does not give offense—one chooses to take offense.

When I react, I put my serenity in the hands of someone else.

R A T S = Rise Above The Situation And Seek Serenity

SURRENDER

When you get really tired of swimming upstream, just roll over and float.

To Let Go is not to abandon.

Secrets lose their shame when spoken in the light. (– Bob A.)

Release with Love—Open your hands and release your loved one to live their own life.

It's never too soon and it's never too late.

Life is to honor, not to solve.

When you have had enough pain, you will surrender.

Keep your intellect over your emotions.

If things don't go your way, then don't have a way!

Turn your will over to the man who calmed the sea.

I am no longer in charge of the rescue mission for my children.
(– Marge)

Surrender = Freedom.

Surrender makes me spiritually teachable.

Living the steps requires two acts: Faith and Surrender.
(– Carol)

The experiences I am going through are given to me as a gift to help me grow.
(– Thomas)

Some of my kid's issues have my name on them, but all of their solutions have their own name on them. (– Eileen)

I am a survivor not a savior—my love cannot save the ones I love.

Bring your body to a meeting and your head will follow.

THE DISEASE

Alcoholism never stops—it's just given a daily reprieve.
(– Oren)

Is what I am doing enhancing my recovery or am I spreading the disease in my family?
(– Oren)

One person drinks and six people are directly affected.

An egomaniac and a people pleaser are the same thing. (– Bill)

When the shit hits the fan—don't catch it; duck. (– Jack)

Alcoholism is an equal opportunity illness. (– Oren)

If you start out with an alcoholic and take away the alcohol you end up with the "IC." (– Oren)

As much as the alcohol grew, that is as much as my disease grew. (– Stephanie)

This is a disease of amnesia.

Don't collaborate with the disease by enabling.

If you take the alcohol out of the alcoholism, what you have left is the ISM, or "in-side-mess."

Alcoholism is not just a spectator sport—eventually the whole family gets to participate.

You don't have to drink to suffer from alcoholism.

THE JOURNEY, THE GROWTH

If you could ask the beautiful butterfly to speak, ask her if she regretted being the ugly worm? (– Judy)

Short-term decisions have long-term ramifications.

A virtue taken to the extreme is a character defect. (– Julie)

I have the power over what goes in my mouth, what comes out of my mouth, and what stays in my head. (– Lauren)

If I don't have the courage to start, I've already finished.

Breakdown can create breakthroughs.

Things fall apart so things can fall together.

I've learned to shut the trap door before I fall into it—again.

Don't give in to "sheet therapy." (– Jerry)

The time you spend wasting is not wasted.

Obsession is mental abuse. (– Mary)

Glitches happen in life and when they do, we show our true character. (– Jay)

So much has been given me that I have not time to ponder what has been denied. (– Helen Keller)

Surrender means going over to the winning side.

There is no pain in change; the pain comes in the resistance to the change. (– Eric)

Every flower must grow through dirt. (– Jane)

Hardship is the pathway to peace.

Lack of change is lack of growth

The longer I live, the more I realize how little I know, and that there are no absolutes. (– Corinne)

A problem can stop me, but a challenge is just a roadblock.

3 A's = Awareness, Acceptance, Action

He who finds himself loses his misery.

Grief is not gracious. (– Joan R.)

Life has meaning only in the struggles.

A F G E = Another Fucking Growth Experience. (– Carol)

If I don't go forward, I don't stand still—I go backwards.

I am no longer the cosmic concierge of the world—making sure everyone is comfortable and taken care of. (– Oren)

Do I expect healthy behavior from unhealthy people?

Growth comes in the quiet space between what was and what has yet to come.

Celebrate the struggles for they give birth to the growth.

Triumph or defeat is in the hands of God.

Today, there is nothing good, nor anything bad in my life.
Today, there are only things that will help me to grow.
(– Kathy M.)

Making a living is only the first step, but for many people it is the entire journey.

To grow as a human being is to pass from passion to compassion.

Brokenness is not a stumbling block, but rather a steppingstone.
(– John)

The gift of true friendship is that it takes us by the hand and reminds us that we are not alone on the journey.

Life is a journey, not a crash landing.

Pain is inevitable, but suffering is optional.

Be part of the solution, not part of the problem.

Recovery is as much about unlearning as learning.

Inch by inch, life's a cinch; Yard by yard, life is hard.

Keep it green and grow. (– Angel)

We can have emotional sobriety, no matter what our loved ones are doing. (– Oren)

The only one who can love me the way I need to be loved is—me. (– ODAT)

THE PROGRAM

I am grateful when my instincts go to my program first.
(– Tom)

Steps 1–3 = Give it up.
Steps 4–6 = Own up.
Steps 7–9 = Make Up.
Steps 10–12 = Keep It Up.

It takes what it takes and all that it takes to get here and it takes what it takes and all that it takes to stay here. (– Shirley)

Al-Anon right-sizes our problems. (– Gail)

How are you growing your Program? (– Brock)

Plan A is to get to a meeting; Plan B is to let everything else happen.

Rise above your basic instincts and live free through the wisdom of the 12 steps.

The Elevator to recovery is out of order; Please use the steps.

If I'm focused on the problem, then the problem grows. If I'm focused on my recovery then my recovery grows. (– Stacy)

Coming to a meeting is a spiritual chiropractic session so I can get my head adjusted.

Al-Anon has made me prettier on the inside. (– Kathleen)

The 4th Step is an archeological dig for myself. (– Shannon)

The 5th Step is the beginning of the end of isolation.

I thought my life would be ideal. It ended up an ordeal and I came to Al-Anon to get a new deal. (– Lynn)

Recovery—No one can do it for you and you can't do it alone. (– Andy)

The 12 steps changed my Life but God makes Happy, Joyous, and Free. (– Ray)

Sometimes when drinking from the fountain of Recovery, I drink the water. Sometimes I gargle and sometimes I stumble against the stones of the fountain.

Seven days without a meeting makes one weak.

Pain is inevitable; Pain is optional.

Recovery—Trust God, Clean House, Help Others.

There is a wrench for every nut that walks into these rooms.
(– Walt)

Many Meetings. Many choices.
Few meetings. Few choices.
No meetings. No choices.

It took many years and many miles to get where I am, but it's not many years and many miles to get out—it's only 12 Steps.
(– Todd)

Whether the world hands me a bombshell or a bouquet, I have a moment of sanity where I can stop, think, and use my program.
(– Oren)

Carry the message, not the mess.

If it's about them, we are screwed. (– Janine)

Meeting-makers make it!

Alcoholics—Toxic, mood altering relatives. (– Oren)

A good program reads easy, but works hard. (– Jennifer)

In Al-Anon we learn to listen and we listen to learn.

While we never graduate from Al-Anon we do get a P H D: Peace, Happiness, & Direction.

Live in the solution, not in the problem

Recovery is about being disloyal to dysfunction and loyal to functionality.

Recovery is in the returning to the rooms.

Recovery is in the reruns of the Steps—over and over again.

Al-Anon'ers have an addiction and it is to interfere in other people's lives.

The "Principles" help us to negotiate life.

If we don't treat—we repeat.

I am powerless over nouns and pronouns. (– Jean)

AL-Anon takes sorrow and distills it into inspiration.

All progress must grow from a seed of self-appreciation.

P R O G R A M = People Relying On God To Relay A Message

Progress not perfection

Al-Anon Meetings are the spiritual equivalent of curling up by a roaring fire. (– Walter)

H O W = Honest, Open, Willing

Utilize instead of Analyze.

I came for my head, I stayed for my heart, and it saved my ass.
(– Jane)

In the shelter of each other we live. (– Sr. Rose)

Recovery confers dignity on each one of us.

Life is an obstacle course and Al-Anon helps us to maneuver around the obstacles.

It's so easy when it is easy. (– Ethel)

Progress not perfection

Al-Anon is my launching pad.

THE TWELVE TRADITIONS

1. Our common welfare should come first; personal progress for the greater number depends upon unity.

   This tradition helped me to see that I had a whole family, not just one sick drug addict son, on whom I totally focused and expected everyone else to focus on and help. It helped me to rethink what was best for the whole family and thus began my delivery from codependence. It also helped me to stand strong in what the program was teaching me—to be united in sanity and to use that against the insanity of the disease.

2. For our group purpose there is but one authority-a loving God as He may express Himself in our group conscience. Our leaders are but trusted servants; they do not govern.

   For the first time I saw how a group conscience worked in the rooms. Everyone had a say; everyone was allowed to talk; no one interrupted and then it was put to a vote. Amazing!! I saw my family in a new light—they had rights and they had a right to express themselves. I was not a dictator, not in charge, and not their God. It helped me to be

more fair and to view my family with greater respect and
dignity, regardless of their choices.

3. The relatives of alcoholics, when gathered together for
   mutual aid, may call themselves an Al-Anon Family Group,
   provided that, as a group, they have no other affiliation. The
   only requirement for membership is that there be a problem
   of alcoholism in a friend or relative.

"No other affiliation" meant to me that I didn't have to
"JED," that is, "Justify," "Explain," or "Defend" who
or what I was. It didn't matter my social, economic or
educational credentials—all that mattered was that I was
in the right place, where I could be honest and not judged.
I belonged because someone in my family had a substance
abuse problem. No questions asked, no explanation needed;
acceptance, at last.

4. Each group should be autonomous, except in matters
   affecting another group or Al-Anon or AA as a whole.

This tradition gave me permission to say "No" to the
people in my life who were asking me for money and to
do things for them that they were very capable of doing
for themselves. I never had the courage to say "No" until

I realized that my family needed to be "autonomous" which means self-supporting—self-supporting financially, physically, emotionally, and spiritually. It also helped me to realize that I was being taken advantage of by alcoholics who continually drained me emotionally and financially. This tradition was a spiritual awakening for me.

5. Each Al-Anon Family Group has but one purpose: to help families of alcoholics. We do this by practicing the 12 steps of AA ourselves, by encouraging and understanding our alcoholic relatives, and by welcoming and giving comfort to the families of alcoholics.

This tradition gave clarify to my purpose in my family and with my friends. I needed to take care of myself, that is, to practice the 12 steps, and then, and only then, could I give encouragement and understanding to others. It also challenged me to give compassion and not hatred and anger. It helped me to view the alcoholic with new eyes, and a softer heart.

6. Our Al-Anon Family Groups ought never endorse, finance, or lend our name to any outside enterprise, lest problems of money, property and prestige divert us from our primary spiritual aim. Although a separate entity, we should always cooperate with AA.

And I should never endorse, finance, or lend my name to any of the crazy, manipulative schemes my alcoholics threw at me. Nor should I bankroll any of the numerous requests that my still sick friends asked of me. It is not my job to help their enterprises, all of them destructive by the way. My focus has to be on my primary aim—my spiritual aim. My job is spiritual growth and my teacher is my Higher Power and the Program.

7. Every group ought to be fully self-supporting, declining outside contributions.

This taught me the importance of making it on one's own—self-supporting in all ways. By enabling, I was crippling. This also helped me to learn to say "No." It also helped me to realize that I could not fix or help every newcomer that walked through the doors of Al-Anon. They, like me, had to be self-supporting, and so I declined trying to be their main contributor—that is best left to their Higher Power.

8. Al-Anon 12-step work should remain forever nonprofessional, but our service centers may employ special workers.

This tradition evens the playing field. It doesn't matter if I am a professional or if you are a professional—we are all equal in the rooms and our professions are left outside the door. It also helped me to realize that I could employ special workers, or professionals, outside of the program that would enhance and help my recovery. It opened my mind to other ways of recovery both for myself and for my family.

9. Our groups, as such, ought never be organized: but we may create service boards or committees directly responsible to those we serve.

And so, as in Al-Anon, my family can never be organized, like a club or formal organization, but we have an obligation to one another. The obligation is that each family member is accountable to the family for their behavior and they need to act responsibly for the sake of the family. I learned that unacceptable behavior from a family member was not acceptable and if it was bad for the family I had to set boundaries and not tolerate it. It was the beginning of detachment for me.

10. The Al-Anon Family Groups have no opinion on outside issues hence our name ought never be drawn into public controversy.

This helped me to not have opinions; that is, judgments and criticisms of other people. It helped me to "Live and Let

Live" and not to continually take my family's inventory. In minding my own business, I am less likely to be drawn back into the controversies that go on in my family between my kids, my grandkids, and my extended family.

11. Our public relations policy is based on attraction rather than promotion; we need always maintain personal anonymity at the level of press, radio, TV, and films. We need guard with special care the anonymity of all AA members.

I knew through this tradition that if I wanted my family to "get" the program I better make it attractive, so I stop ramming it down their throats and stop reciting slogans and pages in *One Day At A Time*. I started to walk the walk and not just talk the talk. I learned that the best sermon ever preached was the sermon that was lived, and I tried to live it.

The other part of this tradition that taught me volumes was the anonymity part. I finally realized that my alcoholics and drug addicts were entitled to the dignity of their choices and that I had no right to broadcast their story to anyone who would listen. I had violated their anonymity many times, before I learned this lesson.

12. Anonymity is the spiritual foundation of all our Traditions, ever reminding us to place principles above personalities.

Anonymity is not only to protect our identity. In some cases, for those living in abusive situations, it is to protect their lives. I have seen the panic of woman who fear that their anonymity will be broken and their lives would be in jeopardy and for that reason I am fiercely protective of everyone's right to privacy and anonymity.

Possibly the greatest aid of all to me is the last part of this tradition. In so many instances I am able to tell myself to "place principles above personalities." This has helped me to accept people for who they are and to rise above their humanness and flaws. In my family I am able to remember, when we are all together for some event, to enjoy the moment, celebrate the occasion, and disregard the many personalities that are all playing tug of war.

It has helped me innumerable times to "celebrate the best and forget the rest."

The above is not conference approved and only the opinion of the person who wrote it. (– Charlene)

WISDOM

We have no friends named "What If" or "If Only."

I'll know what I am meant to know, when I am meant to know it.

Say what you mean, mean what you say, but don't say it mean.

There is more wisdom in your spirit than in your head.

Life is like licking the honey off a thorn.

Keep the "I" over the "E"—the Intellect over the Emotion.

The thought comes from the feeling.

We don't have to J E D = Justify, Explain, and Defend.

"No" is a full and complete sentence.

Principles above personalities

What is a bad man but a good teacher.

Defending depletes *my* energy—not the other person's!

The entire sum of existence is the magic of being needed by just one person.

Life is a journey, not a destination.

Stay in the moment—keep your head where your feet are.

To remember the good and forget the rest—that is the dictate of wisdom.

I have never in my life learned anything from any man who agreed with me. (– Erick)

Smart people learn from their mistakes, but wise people learn from other people's mistakes.

If it's hysterical, it is historical.

An overreaction comes from a wounded place.

Luck is when opportunity meets hard work.

Do it smarter, not harder.

The first response to interruption in my life is resistance, but in the interruption is the challenge, the call, the voice of God, and the growth experience. (– John)

This, too, shall pass.

There is no such thing as a healthy extreme.

What others think of me is none of my business.

You cannot build a tree. It has to grow—inch by inch—it is a process, like our life.
(– Andy)

Inch by inch, life's a cinch. Yard by yard, life is hard.

One Day at a time.

Wisdom comes from a heart of faith, not from a *headful* of facts.

The little sheep stays with the flock for one reason—self-preservation. (– Maurice)

Trust is valid, based on verification. (– Michelle)

When you're lost in the forest at night . . . that is not the time to find your way out. Wait for the sunshine to come in and for the darkness to leave. (– Mike)

Nothing is worth my full and complete attention. (– Lisa)

Our lives are like an EKG—we have ups and downs, but if we have flat lines we are dead!

The tree that won't bend breaks and the tree that bends too much breaks. (– Karen)

A wise man opens his mouth when he has something to say; a fool opens his mouth because he has to say something.
(– Andy)

Intimacy = In To Me, See?

T H I N K = is it: Thoughtful, Honest, Intelligent, Necessary, and Kind?

We see things not as *they* are; we see things as *we* are.

Do not paint this day with the experience of yesterday.

Giving always moves in circles . . . when you give, you receive.

To be rich is to know you have enough.

If you don't make peace with whatever is bothering you, you'll never have peace. (– John)

I am a survivor, not a savior.

I am a survivor and a thriver.

Anything that is urgent is rarely important and anything that is important is rarely urgent. (– Jim)

My life is S H I T = Simply How I Think!

W A I T = Why Am I Talking?

I can journalize; I don't have to verbalize.

Whoever fights monsters beware not to become a monster. (courage to change)

It is our expectations, not the other person that usually lets us down.

Once is a fluke; twice is a coincidence; three times is a pattern.

Make Myself Available to Life.

Q - T I P = Quit Taking It Personally

It never gets darker than midnight. (– Adrian)

Everyone has a piece of wisdom.

There are two kinds of business—*my* business and *none* of my business.

If you are what you do, then when you don't, you aren't. (– Roxie)

An insult is not an insult unless I accept it.

I am enough; I have enough; I do enough.

Experience is not what happens *to* you; experience is what you *do* with what happens to you.

WORRY

Worry: A thin stream of thought that left to its own devices will turn into a raging river of fear. (– Vicky)

Worry: An endless circle of fear around a pivot of doubt. (– Lorene)

If you worry, why pray? And if you pray, why worry? (– Liz)

Worrying is paying interest on troubles that may never come due. (– Todd)

Worrying is praying for bad things to happen.

Turn off the projector!

Sometimes I have to make the right decision and sometimes I have to make the decision right. (– Carol)

Worrying is like a rocking chair . . . It gives you something to do, but it gets you nowhere.

Worry never changed one thing about tomorrow, it simply ruined today.

Worry saps your serenity and your energy.

Worry and Hope cannot coexist.

• • •

INDEX

Abuse 1
Acceptance. 3
Addiction. 11
Advise 7
Advice, Learning, Teaching 7
Alcoholism. 11
Alcoholism, Addiction. . . 11
Amends 13
Amends, Anonymity, Attitude
. . . . 13
Anger 15
Anonymity. 13
Attitude 13
Change 17
Character Defects 21
Codependence 27
Control 33
Courage 29
Dedication v
Defects, Character 21
Denial 33
Denial, Control. 33
Detachment 37
Disease, Insanity of the . . 71
Disease, The 113
Faith 39

Fear. 43
Focus on Yourself 47
Forgiveness 51
God. 53
Gratitude. 61
Growth, The 115
Happiness 63
Hope 65
Humor 69
Humor, Humility. 69
Humility 69
Insanity of the Disease. . . 71
Journey, The 115
Judgment. 73
Learning 7
Let It Begin with Me. . . . 75
Living in the Moment . . . 79
Love 81
Mind My Own Business. . 85
Miscellaneous 89
Negativism. 93
Prayer 95
Prayer, Serenity 105
Preface ix
Program, The 121
Resentment. 97

Resentment, Shame 97
Self-Love. 101
Serenity 107
Serenity Prayer. 105
Serenity, Spirituality. . . 107
Shame 97
Spirituality. 107
Surrender. 111
Table of Contents vii
Teaching 7

The Disease 113
The Journey 115
The Journey, The Growth 115
The Program. 121
The Twelve Traditions . . 127
Twelve Traditions, The . 127
Traditions, The Twelve . 127
Wisdom 135
Worry 143

Made in United States
Orlando, FL
07 June 2024

47610446R00089